Withstand

WITHSTAND

THE CULTURE WAR IS A SPIRITUAL BATTLE

**RYAN DB KIMMEL &
JONATHAN DELGER**

RESOUND

Resound Publishing

Withstand

Copyright 2024 by Ryan DB Kimmel and Jonathan Delger

All rights reserved. No part of this publication may be reproduced, stored in a retrieval system, or transmitted in any form by any means, electronic, mechanical, photocopy, recording, or otherwise, without the prior permission of the publisher, except as provided for by USA copyright law.

Cover design: Mitchell Leach

Second printing 2024

Printed in the United States of America

Scripture quotations are from the ESV® Bible (The Holy Bible, English Standard Version®), copyright © 2001 by Crossway, a publishing ministry of Good News Publishers. Used by permission. All rights reserved.

ISBN: 979-8-218-55458-3

Websites:
resoundmedia.cc

*To our wives
Tiffany and Stephanie
alongside whom we fight the good fight*

Contents

Introduction	*1*
Chapter 1: Present Darkness vs Spiritual Strength	*7*
Chapter 2: Personal Distraction vs Truth & Righteousness	*17*
Chapter 3: Polarizing Division vs Gospel Peace	*29*
Chapter 4: Spiritual Doubt vs Faith & Salvation	*41*
Chapter 5: Missional Decline vs The Word of God	*51*
Index	*59*

INTRODUCTION

There are moments that remind me...this is not the world I grew up in.

My phone rings.

"Hello?"

"Hey honey, we're on our way home, but I wanted to give you a heads up that we'll need to have a talk with the kids when we get home. It's about something that happened at the grocery store."

As a father of four young children, this is not the first time I've heard the words, "we'll need to have a talk with the kids when we get home." However, since my wife thought it worthy to call ahead, I assume it must be something a little bigger than usual.

Introduction

"Our cashier at the checkout was a gentleman who happened to be wearing a dress and lots of makeup. The kids have lots of questions."

Over the next few minutes, I tried to compile a list in my mind of some relevant biblical truths. This is a man made in God's image. He is living outside God's design. We love him. Like the rest of us, he needs Jesus. We hope for him to one day meet Jesus and walk in his ways.

I then tried to think of how to explain these biblical truths to four children between the ages of 3 and 8. It became a little more complicated.

"Yes, he is a man. No, men don't normally dress that way. Yes, we should love him and treat him with respect. Yes, we do want to tell him about Jesus and what the Bible says. No, trying to explain it to him over the counter at the checkout, while he is working and there are lots of people around, might not be the best approach. No, I wasn't planning to go back and tell him later."

"Honestly, no, I don't have a plan, and I'm not sure how I was going to speak the truth in love to this man letting – him know that we care about him – and that because we care about him, we want to share the truth with him: the truth about sin and judgment:

about how he can have salvation through Jesus: about how God's design is better than everything the world is telling him: about, at this moment in history, it would seem society has lost its epistemological and moral footing: and that we really need some change."

Some have said that we are in the midst of a culture war. The United States is more divided now than perhaps ever before. We disagree on significant issues such as climate change, abortion, gun laws, separation of power, immigration, public education, Israel, Ukraine, marijuana, gay marriage, transgenderism, taxes, and more. Not only do we disagree at the surface level of policy, we disagree at the level of values, morals, facts, and worldview.

Like I said, some have called this a culture war. However, I'm here to tell you this is not just a culture war…this is a spiritual battle.

For the time is coming when people will not endure sound teaching, but having itching ears they will accumulate for themselves teachers to suit their own passions, and will turn away from listening to the truth and wander off into myths (2 Timothy 4:3-4).

The Bible tells us that people will stray from the truth and that false teachers will be part of that. But in another letter by the same apostle, we are told basically the same thing from another perspective.

Now the Spirit expressly says that in later times some will depart from the faith by devoting themselves to deceitful spirits and teachings of demons (1 Timothy 4:1).

Let me share one more passage that makes this point as well. (To clarify something that could be confusing in this next passage, "the god of this world" is one way the Bible sometimes refers to Satan.)

In their case the god of this world has blinded the minds of the unbelievers, to keep them from seeing the light of the Gospel of the glory of Christ, who is the image of God (2 Corinthians 4:4).

Now some of you might be thinking - "Come on pastor, I'm too old for the boogeyman. Don't over-spiritualize the situation. This is just people with bad ideas. Are you really trying to tell me there are spiritual forces at work here?"

That's exactly what I'm trying to tell you. For generations, Christians have named three primary enemies of God's people: the world, the flesh, and the devil. However, in some circles – and in this cultural moment in particular – many of us have forgotten to consider this third enemy.

We are two pastors who are concerned by what we see in the world around us, but are perhaps equally concerned by how we see the church responding. As an antidote, we propose not something new, but something very, very old. God has given his people ancient armor to stand against the schemes of the devil (Ephesians 6:10-20). With one eye on the Bible and one eye on the culture, we aim, through the following chapters, to equip Christians to put on the whole armor of God and to withstand in the evil day.

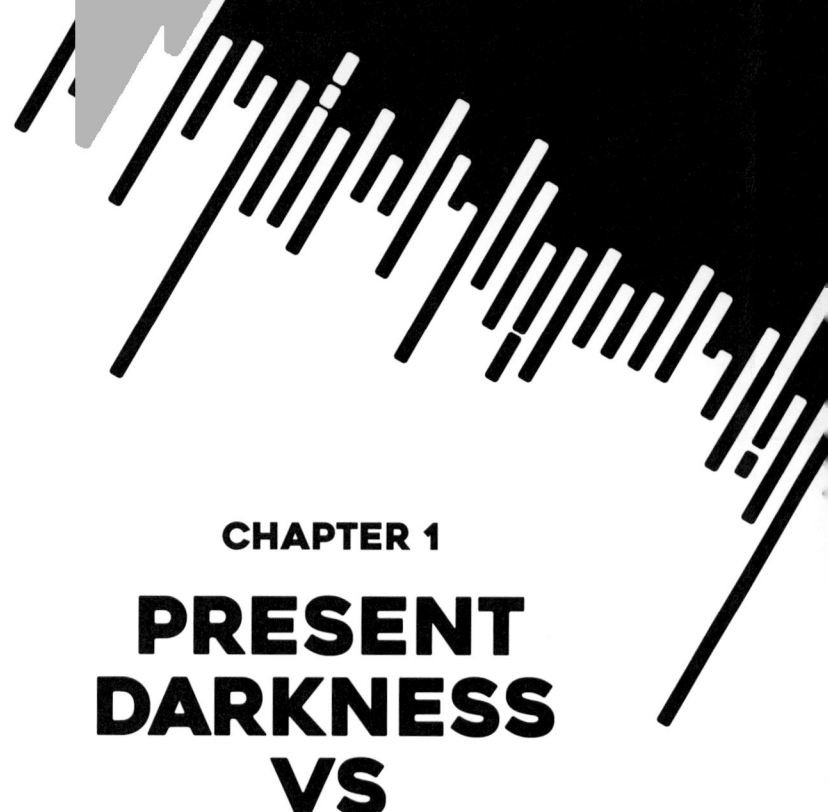

CHAPTER 1

PRESENT DARKNESS VS SPIRITUAL STRENGTH

Finally, be strong in the Lord and in the strength of his might. Put on the whole armor of God, that you may be able to stand against the schemes of the devil. For we do not wrestle against flesh and blood, but against the rulers, against the authorities, against the cosmic powers over this present darkness, against the spiritual forces of evil in the heavenly places. Therefore take up the whole armor of God, that you may be able to withstand in the evil day, and having done all, to stand firm.
— *Ephesians 6:10-13*

If we are to stand strong, then we need the whole armor of God

In a single week, I received each of the following text messages from couples within the church. "Things are falling apart. I'm pretty sure there is no fixing this." "Is it really marriage if I can't trust my spouse? Pastor, would you be willing to meet with us?" "Can we get together? We are really struggling right now and aren't sure how long we can keep this up."

Even for Christian couples, marriage is hard. The whole Christian life is hard. I wonder, did anyone tell them that when they got started?

The Battle Is Real
The Bible is quite clear that the Christian life is a battle, not a stroll in the park.

Be strong...stand firm...put on the whole armor...we do not wrestle against flesh and blood...but against the cosmic powers over this present darkness (Ephesians 6:10-13).

Christians are challenged to suffer as soldiers (2 Timothy 2:3), to stay focused on our mission like soldiers (2 Timothy 2:4), and Christians brothers are referred to as fellow soldiers (Philippians 2:25).

As soldiers of Christ, our mission can be stated in two simple parts: be faithful disciples and make more disciples. We are to put our faith in Jesus (John 3:16), fight hard against sin (Romans 8:13), and strive to walk in the ways of the Lord (John 14:15). We are also called to share the good news of salvation through Jesus with others so that they can be saved and walk with Him (Matthew 28:18-20).

In the battle of the Christian life, we have opposition. There are forces that want to stop us from being faithful disciples and making more disciples. These forces come from inside of us as well as outside of us.

The problem is…many Christians don't realize they are in a battle. Are you aware that you are in a battle? Are you alert to the forces working against you?

There is currently a video on YouTube by the nation's largest provider of sex education entitled "What is Virginity?".[1] The video is set in a classroom complete with a teacher's desk, chalkboard, and "Sex Ed 101" written on the wall. The following are just a few quotes spoken by the teacher featured in the video.

> *Virginity is a completely made up concept. It's a term that was created simply to control and shame people - mainly women.*

Another reason the idea of virginity is whack, is that sex means different things to different people.

It's time to throw away the notion of "losing your virginity"! What if instead of "losing" something we reframe it as "gaining"? Because, the truth is, when we make our own decision to become sexually active, we aren't setting ourselves up to lose anything at all! We hope we are gaining things like intimacy, self insight, pleasure, and empowerment.

Are you aware of the messages coming at you? Are you aware of how they contradict the Bible? Are you aware of the danger they present to you, your family, your church, and the world?

If you are not aware that you are in a battle, then you have already lost.

The Enemy Is Real

Late one night, I called my wife, who was my girlfriend at the time and working at a restaurant. I left a voicemail for her to hear when her shift ended. As I was leaving the voicemail, I had a very strange experience that I have always struggled to describe to others. The best way I can describe it is by sharing what my wife heard on the other end when she finally listened to the voicemail...multiple voices screaming. I was alone when I left that voicemail, yet clearly I was not alone.

For we do not wrestle against flesh and blood, but against the rulers, against the authorities, against the cosmic powers over this present darkness, against the spiritual forces of evil in the heavenly places (Ephesians 6:12).

What are these rulers, authorities, powers, and forces? The intention of this passage is not to give us a hierarchy of hell or an organizational chart of the demonic, but in short, these words refer to Satan's demonic army.

While the Bible doesn't give us great detail about the inner workings of the unseen spiritual realm, we do get glimpses. One story that has always astounded me is in Daniel 10. I encourage you to read the whole story in your Bible, but I will quote part of it here.

Fear not, Daniel, for from the first day that you set your heart to understand and humbled yourself before your God, your words have been heard, and I have come because of your words. The prince of the kingdom of Persia withstood me twenty-one days, but Michael, one of the chief princes, came to help me, for I was left there with the kings of Persia, and came to make you understand what is to happen to your people in the latter days. For the vision is for days yet to come. (Daniel 10:12-14).

So, to try to summarize: Daniel saw a vision and prayed to God. God sent an angel (most likely Gabriel) to speak to Daniel, but he was held up by a demon prince. So, the archangel Michael came to help fight the demon so that Gabriel could go to Daniel, Gabriel delivers encouragement to Daniel, but then has to go back to rejoin the fight with Michael against the demon prince. What!?

We may not know a lot about the war in the unseen realm, but it is real. Despite this truth plainly portrayed in the Bible, Gallup polls tell us that Americans' belief in the demonic is steadily declining and that Americans are less likely to believe in the demonic than in God, angels, heaven, or hell.[2]

There is a famous old hymn that has always struck me because of the respect that it shows to Satan.

For still our ancient foe
doth seek to work us woe.
His craft and power are great
and armed with cruel hate.
On earth is not his equal.

It once struck me as so strange for a Christian hymn writer to say of Satan - on earth is not his equal. However, over time, I have come to realize that this is really true.

And the great dragon was thrown down, that ancient serpent, who is called the devil and Satan, the deceiver of the whole world—he was thrown down to the earth, and his angels were thrown down with him… "woe to you, O earth and sea, for the devil has come down to you in great wrath, because he knows that his time is short" (Revelation 12:7-12).

The enemy is powerful, dangerous, and clever. The enemy has schemes, or schema, or strategies (Ephesians 6:11). Like a good football coach, he has watched the tape. He knows our movements and recognizes our patterns. He has planned to capitalize on our weaknesses. He is like a great predator on the prowl.

Be sober-minded; be watchful. Your adversary the devil prowls around like a roaring lion, seeking someone to devour (1 Peter 5:8).

The enemy has a strategy to beat you. Do you have a strategy to resist him?

There is one last very important point to be made

here about our enemy - our enemy is not flesh and blood (Ephesians 6:12).

Perhaps one of the most effective strategies of the enemy at this cultural moment is to make us think that other people are our enemy. If we fight against our neighbor instead of Satan, then Satan has already won.

Your neighbor is not your enemy. Your battle is not against flesh and blood. Yes, there are people playing for the wrong team right now. But they are actually captives, not enemies (Luke 4:18). We should pity them, pray for them, love them, and share the Gospel with them. Our desire is for their freedom, not their destruction.

So, What Do We Do?
Christians, we are in a battle. This battle has an impact on our culture, our friends, our families, and our churches. But this battle is not primarily cultural. It is primarily spiritual. If we want to take part in this fight, we need to engage with it not merely on the surface, but at the underlying spiritual level. So how do we do that?

Put on the whole armor of God, that you may be able to stand against the schemes of the devil (Ephesians 6:10).

The very next verse in that famous hymn I mentioned earlier goes like this:

> *Did we in our own strength confide,*
> *our striving would be losing.*
> *Were not the right Man on our side,*
> *the Man of God's own choosing.*
> *Dost ask who that may be?*
> *Christ Jesus, it is He!*

We are not meant to fight this great battle against this great enemy on our own. We are to do it in the power of Christ.

How do we fight in the power of Christ? He tells us : by putting on the whole armor of God. Not part of the armor – we are to put on the full and complete armor of God.

That is what the rest of this book is about.

CHAPTER 2

PERSONAL DISTRACTION VS TRUTH & RIGHTEOUSNESS

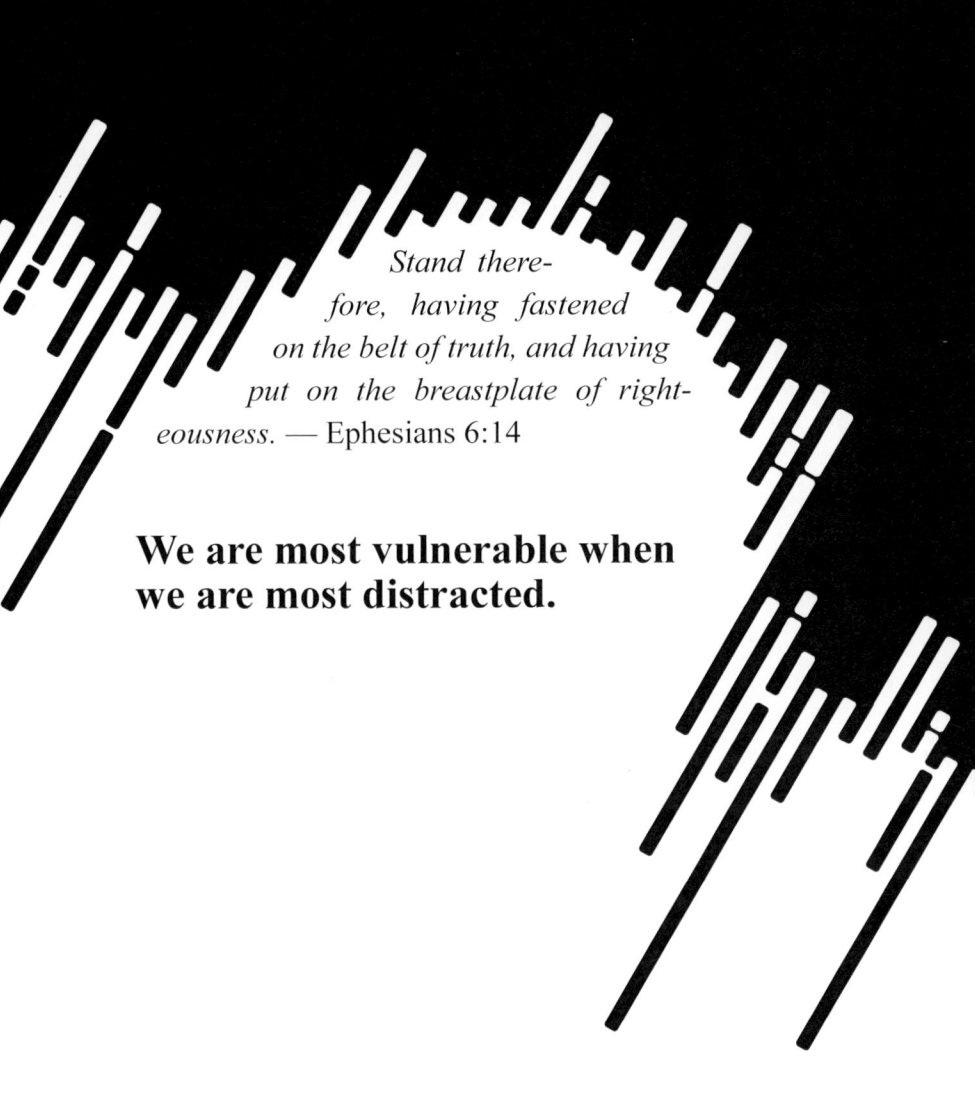

Stand therefore, having fastened on the belt of truth, and having put on the breastplate of righteousness. — Ephesians 6:14

We are most vulnerable when we are most distracted.

Did you know that the civilization we know as the Ancient Roman Empire wasn't always an empire? It was once a republic. At one time, power resided with the people rather than with a single man. How did the people lose their power? In the words of the ancient poet Juvenal - *"The people that once bestowed commands, consulships, legions, and all else, now concerns itself no more, and longs eagerly for just two things: bread and circuses"*[3]

In the words of Juvenal, the answer is simple: the people were willing to give up their power as long as they had food and entertainment, as long as they were satisfied or pacified.

Unfortunately, the same is often true for us. We will let the world come to ruin around us as long as we can eat snacks and watch television in the privacy of our own homes. Keep us distracted and we will give up our influence.

Actually, the problem is worse than that. When we are distracted, not only will we give up our influence in the world, we will surrender the defenses of our own minds and hearts (and those of our families) to the influence of the world.

Attention Is The Antidote For Distraction
God calls us to stand, but the enemy wants us to fall. Have you ever heard the saying, 'the devil is trying

to trip you up?' This is true, but actually the Bible tells us his ambitions are far worse. He doesn't merely want us to trip, he wants to devour us. "Your adversary the devil prowls around like a roaring lion, seeking someone to devour" (1 Peter 5:8).

God calls us to stand...to be established, to be steadfast, to hold our ground. So, why are so many falling? Is it because they turn from fiercely fighting the enemy to fiercely fighting their God? Is it because of apostasy? Or is it because of apathy?

In America, one of the greatest tools the devil uses to make us fall is distraction.

My wife and I love to play chess. I am a strong chess player, but my wise wife knows that if we sit so that I can see the TV in the next room while we play, then she will win every time. When I'm distracted, my attention is divided, I am entertained or engaged elsewhere: then, I am less engaged in what matters. This makes me an easy target.

So, where are you distracted? When is your attention divided so that you become an easy target? When are you pacified by entertainment so that you don't put up any resistance to the devil's schemes? When are you satisfied with the pleasures of this life so that you don't focus on what matters for eternity?

Divide and conquer is a military strategy. Jesus said it himself, "no city or house divided against itself will stand" (Matthew 12:25). Is your attention divided against itself? Is your time, energy, money, mind, or heart divided? How then will you stand?

We are distracted primarily in two ways: by the lies of the world and by the desires of our heart. These two vulnerabilities are exactly what the first two pieces of God's armor aim to protect.

Truth Is The Antidote For Deception

When the Apostle Paul (under the inspiration of the Holy Spirit) wrote of armor, he would have been thinking of the armor of a Roman soldier. While we would normally envision a belt going around the outside of an outfit to hold it all together, the belt of a Roman soldier actually went underneath their armor and supported everything.

This is precisely what the belt of truth does. It undergirds and supports everything else. It is because truth plays such a foundational role in our lives that Satan has a war on truth.

Why do you not understand what I say? It is because you cannot bear to hear my word. You are of your father the devil, and your will is to do your father's desires. He was a murderer from the beginning, and does not stand in the truth, because there is no truth in him. When he lies, he speaks out of his own character, for he is a liar and the father of lies. But because I tell the truth, you do not believe me (John 8:43-45).

This passage reveals a lot about what we see in the culture war happening around us. Satan is the Father of lies. Lies flow from his very character. Those poisoned by his lies struggle to believe or even hear the truth.

One of Satan's lies that has deeply impacted our culture is this: truth is whatever works for you. Or, to say it another way: all truth is relative, and there is no absolute truth. 'Truth is different for every person. I have my truth, you have yours, and you can't tell me that my truth is wrong.'

Now, if you ever confront someone who is bold enough to state their position like that, there is an easy defense that is as old as the philosopher Socrates. "Is that true for you or true for me?" The statement, "all truth is relative," is actually a self-defeating statement. It asserts that it is absolutely true that there is no such thing as absolute truth.

Despite the fact that their argument doesn't hold up to the rules of logic, many are still captive to this way of thinking. To give an example: this is why, despite the teachings of biology or the Bible, some people claim that there is no difference between a man and a woman, that one can change their gender, or that gender is a made-up concept all together.

Tragically, the lives of many people made in God's image are being deeply damaged by these deceptions of Satan. Real people are shackled and chained by Satan's lies.

By contrast, Jesus tells us that the truth will set us free.

If you abide in my word, you are truly my disciples, and you will know the truth, and the truth will set you free (John 8:31-32).

Jesus even says that he is truth.

I am the way, and the truth, and the life. No one comes to the Father except through me. (John 14:6)

The antidote for deception is the truth of God's Word.

Blessed is the man who walks not in the counsel of the wicked, nor stands in the way of sinners, nor sits in the seat of scoffers; but his delight is in the law of the Lord, and on his law he meditates day and night (Psalm 1:1-2).

If we want to stand and fight Satan's lies, we must be in God's Word. We must know and understand the truth so that we can identify, repel, and dismantle lies. We must know God's Word so that we can help free others held captive by lies.

Let me say something crazy: We should be reading and reflecting on God's Word every day. The Psalmist said day and night, and I'm just saying every day. I'm taking it easy on you!

Are you reading and reflecting on God's Word every day so that you are equipped in your mind to fight the lies? Are you meditating on God's Word daily so that you have the heart of Jesus to fight lies not with hate, but with love for those held captive?

Righteousness Is The Antidote For Dishonor

For an ancient Roman soldier, the breastplate would have been a large piece of metal worn across the chest. What vital organ did it protect? It protected what we still consider today to be the most important organ: the heart.

In physical terms, we consider the heart to be of highest importance because of its role as the central power station to the body. Likewise, in spiritual terms, we consider the heart to be the central station of desire. If we are to walk in righteousness, we must protect our heart.

Unfortunately, the Bible gives us some bad news about our heart. "The heart is deceitful above all things, and desperately sick" (Jeremiah 17:9). One of the challenges of protecting our heart is that it is already damaged.

Ever since Adam and Eve ate from the tree, sin has had a corrupting influence on the hearts of human beings. Our desires are no longer pure. God designed our hearts to desire righteousness, but because they are damaged, we desire sin. God designed our hearts to desire Him, but because they are tainted, we try to fill our longings with other things.

I recently drove past a billboard that read, "Life is short, get a divorce." Can you spot the lie? This billboard sells a popular cultural lie. It claims that life is about personal happiness, that happiness is achieved by satisfying our selfish desires, and that our spouse is either a tool to satisfy these desires or an obstacle to our desires that must be removed. It also sells the lie that you will be happier on the other side of divorce. This is perhaps the easiest lie to disprove. As a pastor, I can also tell you from experience of walking with couples that life is almost never better on the other side of divorce (cases of abuse being the rare exception).

We could talk for hours about the various dimensions of this cultural lie, but let's instead ask another question: Why is this lie so seductive? If it is so easy to uncover the faulty logic, then why are so many deceived? The answer: Because this lie not only appeals to the mind, but also to a warped desire in our heart. We were made for happiness, or as the Bible often calls it, joy. God designed our hearts to desire joy and to find it in God (Psalm 37:4). However, because of sin, our hearts seek joy in all the wrong places. God did design us to have pleasure in marriage, but because marriage is the union of two sinful people...it doesn't come easy.

Simply defined, righteousness is what's right before God. The pursuit of righteousness will protect your heart. Righteousness is also what will ultimately satisfy your heart since that is what God made it to desire. Our minds and hearts have been warped by sin to believe that happiness is found in going our own way, but the truth is that happiness is ultimately found in a relationship with God and in walking God's way. God is not a grumpy, power-hungry, rule-maker. God is good. God is a loving Father. He made you to find joy in righteousness.

When I look at a soldier in uniform, one of the words that comes to mind is honor. A soldier dressed in armor is honorable. A soldier unprepared for duty or disobeying commands is dishonorable. Sin is shameful. Sin brings dishonor on you, your family, and your God.

So, men, how are you protecting your families from dishonor? If my wife asks me to get the kids dressed in the morning, I'll be honest, I don't know where to find their clothes. But men, do you know how to dress your kids in the armor of God? What are you doing to help your family fight lies and worldly desires, know truth, and walk in righteousness?

There is one final thing that you must know about righteousness. Righteousness does not ultimately come from within us; it comes from outside of us. You cannot be right with God or even begin to walk in his ways until you have received the righteousness of Christ.

For our sake he made him to be sin who knew no sin, so that in him we might become the righteousness of God (2 Corinthians 5:21).

For by works of the law no human being will be justified in his sight, since through the law comes knowledge of sin. But now the righteousness of God has been manifested apart from the law, although the Law and the Prophets bear witness to it — the righteousness of God through faith in Jesus Christ for all who believe. For there is no distinction: for all have sinned and fall short of the glory of God, and are justified by his grace as a gift, through the redemption that is in Christ Jesus (Romans 3:20-24).

Jesus lived the perfect life that we could not live (Hebrews 4:15), he died the death for sin that we deserved to die (Romans 6:23), and he was raised from the dead so that we too could have new life through faith in him (Romans 4:24-25). When we put our faith in Jesus, we become clothed in his righteousness. Instead of our sin, the Father looks at us and sees Jesus' righteousness.

In response to what God has done for us, not in order to earn it, do we seek to live a righteous life (Ephesians 2:8-10). It is only after we have received the free gift of God's grace that we can, out of love for God, pursue righteous living.

CHAPTER 3

POLARIZING DIVISION VS GOSPEL PEACE

as shoes for your feet, having put on the readiness given by the Gospel of peace.
— Ephesians 6:15

The Gospel makes us ready to bring peace in a polarized world.

Climate change, abortion, gun laws, separation of power, immigration, public education, Israel, Ukraine, marijuana, gay marriage, transgenderism, taxes...need I go on?

Americans are deeply divided, and the polarization is only getting worse.

What is the first thing you think about a person when you see them? Today, we tend to quickly notice clues to a person's position on a political issue, and then we think we know everything about them.

As Christians, the first thing we think of any person we see should be this - there is a person made in the image of God (Genesis 1:27). Until we see the humanity in people before we see the difference in our politics, we will never be the sort of people needed to bring the message of peace to the world.

Yes, politics matter. Don't misunderstand and think that Christians should be neutral in the political sphere. There are moral issues at stake. The well-being of a whole nation of people is at stake. The word "politics" is derived from the ancient Greek word "polis" meaning city. Politics are simply the affairs of the city, state, or nation. Christians should care about and be involved in politics.

However, Christians are first and foremost ambassadors of the kingdom of heaven (2 Corinthians 5:20). That is where we have our ultimate citizenship and from where we receive our ultimate mission. Our king has given us the Gospel of peace to stand in this world.

The Gospel Is What We Stand On
It's been said: If you don't stand for something, you will fall for anything. So, what do you stand for? What do you stand upon? What is your foundation and core conviction?

When a Roman soldier stood ready to receive a wave of attackers, his feet had to stand firm. His shoes must not slip, slide, or crumble. Scripture tells us that the Gospel is like shoes for our feet.

What is the Gospel? The word "Gospel" means good news. The core message of the Christian faith is the good news of the life, death, and resurrection of Jesus Christ (1 Corinthians 15:1-8). Apart from Christ, humans are enemies of God because of our sin (Romans 5:10). But through faith in Jesus, we can have peace with God.

Therefore, since we have been justified by faith, we have peace with God through our Lord Jesus Christ (Romans 5:1).

Withstand

So, the first way the Gospel brings peace is vertical. It creates peace in our most important relationship: between us and God. This is the foundation of the Christian's life and it should be the foundation of every aspect of our lives.

What is the foundation of your home? We say that we are raising our kids, but what does that mean? When you raise a barn, the first thing you do is lay a foundation. When we raise children, we are helping them develop knowledge, beliefs, habits, and behaviors. We are helping them build a foundation that will carry them through life. But what is the foundation we are helping them to build?

Now therefore fear the LORD and serve him in sincerity and in faithfulness. Put away the gods that your fathers served beyond the River and in Egypt, and serve the LORD. And if it is evil in your eyes to serve the LORD, choose this day whom you will serve, whether the gods your fathers served in the region beyond the River, or the gods of the Amorites in whose land you dwell. But as for me and my house, we will serve the LORD (Joshua 24:14-15).

Can you say with Joshua - "as for me and my house, we will serve the Lord?" Regardless of what your friends, neighbors, even other members of your church are saying, will you stand by the Lord and His

Word? In order to do so, you must have a firm foundation, the foundation of the Gospel.

The Gospel Makes Us Ready To Face The World

When it's time to leave the house, we tell our kids - "Alright, time to go; put your shoes on." Putting on your shoes is a sign you are ready to leave home and face the world.

Until you understand the Gospel and feel the impact of the Gospel in your own life, you are not ready to face the world. You won't be a person who brings peace or who heals the divide; more likely, you will be someone who adds to it.

In the midst of a passage about battle, it seems strange to hear the word "peace." The connection between these words is important. On the one hand, it could be said that peace is the opposite of battle, but on the other hand, it should be said that peace is rarely achieved without battle.

Peace is not merely the absence of conflict. Biblical peace, or "shalom," is a state of being where all things are according to God's good design, where all is right with the world. This state won't come fully until Jesus returns, but Christians are called to pursue it in degrees during this life.

So, let's talk about the world we face and how we carry the Gospel into such a world.

A recent Gallup poll[4] compared the positions of Republicans and Democrats from 20 years ago with where they are today on key issues. Let's consider a sample of three important moral issues.

- Twenty years ago, 46% of Democrats were supportive of same-sex marriage, while today 85% are supportive.

- Twenty years ago, 34% of Republicans were supportive of same-sex marriage, while today 57% are supportive.

- Twenty years ago, approximately 63% of Democrats believed sex outside of marriage was acceptable, while today 82% are accepting.

- Twenty years ago, approximately 50% of Republicans believed sex outside of marriage was acceptable, while today 63% are accepting.

- Twenty years ago, 32% of Democrats believed abortion should be legal under any circumstance, while today 59% believe this.

- Twenty years ago, 15% of Republicans believed abortion should be legal under any circumstance, while today 12% believe this.

There are a few conclusions we can draw from this data. First, neither Republicans nor Democrats represent the kingdom of God. Only the church was designed to be the body of Christ on earth, and even the church is an imperfect body until Christ returns. No other organization can take up the role God designed for his church. Both political parties are made up of fallen human beings, both are full of people who are doing what they think is best for the world, and both fall radically short of God's perfect moral vision for society.

Second (and if this conclusion makes you want to shut the book, stay tuned for the third conclusion), the Democratic Party is more accepting of unbiblical views and practices. When we look at the polling data here and review the party platform (a paper produced each election year that outlines the principles and positions of the party), it is clear that the Democratic Party is drifting farther and faster from God's design than the other party. This is not to say that some Christians can't agree with some of the policies of this party. Rather, this is to simply say that the official stated positions of the party and the majority of those who identify with this party are more accepting of unbiblical views and practices.

Third (and this conclusion will also make some want to shut the book), while the Republican Party is not drifting as far or fast as the Democrats, this party does continue to move away from God's design on several issues. The data clearly shows that, over the last twenty years, Republicans have become more accepting of unbiblical views and practices. One notable exception is that of abortion, for which we can be thankful. In fact, the data actually shows that Republicans today are more accepting of some unbiblical views or practices than Democrats were twenty years ago.

The world we face is deeply divided, but worse yet, the enemy seems to be gaining ground on both sides of the political aisle. Although one party is further down the line, both parties are drifting farther from God's design. This is a spiritual battle.

So, how do we face such a world? How do we carry the Gospel of peace into the world? One important realization for Christians is this: real change won't come through political action alone. Real change must come through heart-change.

Political action by Christians can be valuable. The Bible does not just teach what is best for Christians, it teaches what is best for all human beings. What is best for the world is to operate according to the Creator's design. Christians shouldn't be afraid to stand for biblical principles in the public square because those principles are good for humanity.

Nonetheless, the mission God gave to the church was not for political action; it was to preach the Gospel and make disciples.

Go therefore and make disciples of all nations, baptizing them in the name of the Father and of the Son and of the Holy Spirit, teaching them to observe all that I have commanded you (Matthew 28:19-20).

The Gospel makes our own hearts ready to face the world and it is what we have to offer the world.

The Gospel Carries Us Back Home
At the end of a long day, most of us just want to go home. When soldiers are away at war, many of them are looking forward to going home. Just as my boots carry me back home at the end of the day, so will the Gospel.

There is a hope and peace that come from having a picture of home fastened in our minds. When we know where we are going in the end, it enables us to endure present circumstances. It enables us to stand.

Our ultimate citizenship is in heaven and the Gospel is our ticket home. This is the final way in which the Gospel brings peace. When we are anxious or weary of this divided world, we can fix our eyes on the Gospel and find peace.

Rejoice in the Lord always; again I will say, rejoice. Let your reasonableness be known to everyone. The Lord is at hand; do not be anxious about anything, but in everything by prayer and supplication with thanksgiving let your requests be made known to God. And the peace of God, which surpasses all understanding, will guard your hearts and your minds in Christ Jesus (Philippians 4:4-7).

CHAPTER 4

SPIRITUAL DOUBT VS FAITH & SALVATION

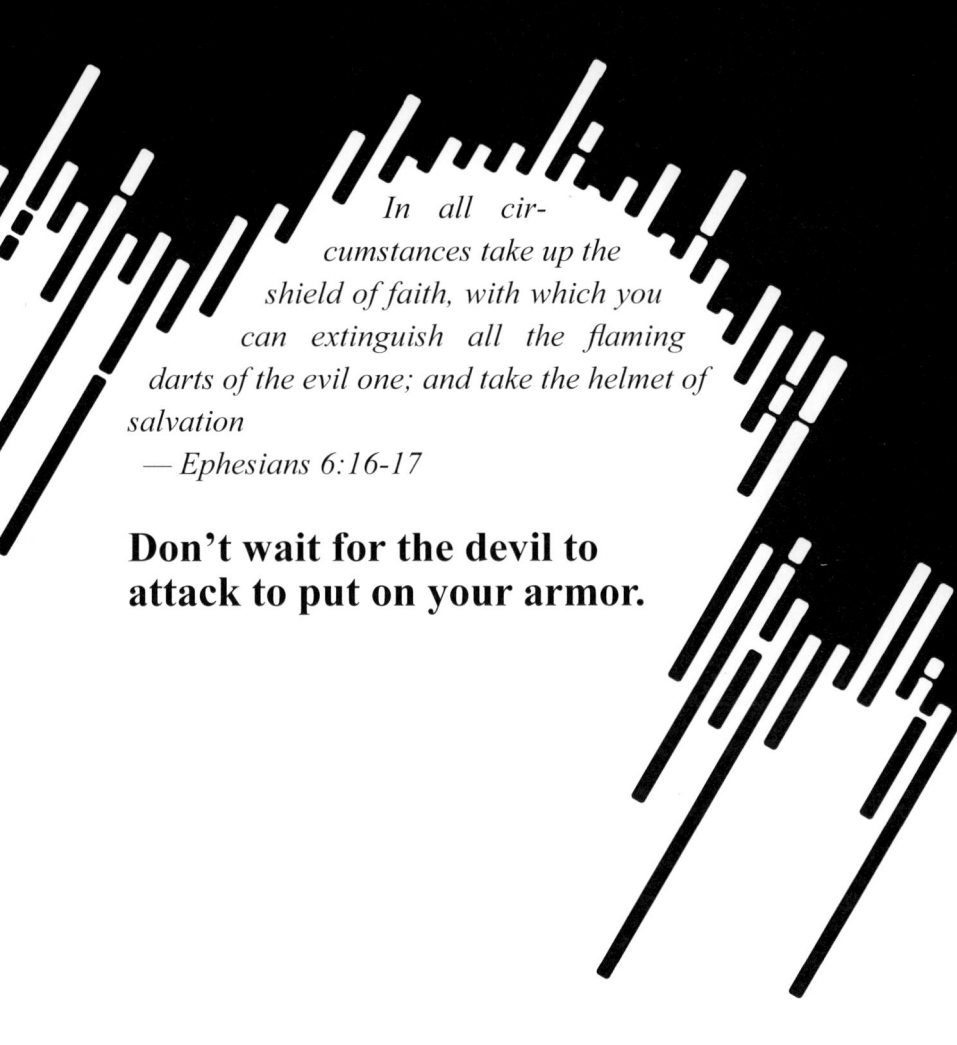

In all circumstances take up the shield of faith, with which you can extinguish all the flaming darts of the evil one; and take the helmet of salvation
— Ephesians 6:16-17

Don't wait for the devil to attack to put on your armor.

Withstand

When you live in Michigan, especially in the winter, it is a good idea to own a generator. Whether from a thunderstorm or a blizzard, the electricity does go out from time to time. When it does, it is convenient to be able to fire up the generator and still use the refrigerator, the microwave, or even the tv. In the winter, it is essential for heat.

So, shortly after we bought our house, I bought a generator. It sat in the garage untouched for about a year before the first time the power went out. When the power finally went out, my wife looked at me and asked the question, "Well, are you going to set up the generator?" My response..."I would, except...I haven't wired the house for it." Fortunately, the power came back on within an hour. I took this as a warning and made a mental note that some weekend in the near future I should probably wire the house for the generator…. yeah...some weekend.

About a year later, this time because of a blizzard, the power went out again. My wife gave me that look and posed the same question as before. Now I would have to convince a friend to come help me wire the house in the dark, in the cold, and with my whole family waiting for the heat to come back on.

Unfortunately, some of us treat God's armor, and our faith, like I treated my generator. We know it's there, but we never use it, so when times get tough, we don't even know how.

Faith Isn't For Passivity; It's For Activity

God says, "In all circumstances take up the shield of faith." In all circumstances: Not just some circumstances, all of them. God's armor is not meant to hang in the closet or sit in the garage.

Those flaming darts of the evil one can come out of nowhere. The devil doesn't give us a warning. Temptation to sin or to doubt God's character comes in many forms: a co-worker who makes you mad enough to hate, a story you heard that is juicy enough to gossip, a situation that is tough enough to lie, or the loss of a loved one that makes you wonder how a good God could let such a thing happen.

The Apostle Paul tells his apprentice Timothy to "fight the good fight of faith" (1 Timothy 6:12). Before his execution, Paul reflected that he had fought the good fight (2 Timothy 4:7). Faith isn't a secondary thing, it is the fight of the Christian life. Unfortunately, many Christians would identify with this song lyric: "I only talk to God when I need a favor, and I only pray when I ain't got a prayer".[5]

Are you under attack by the evil one? If not, it may

be because you have already been defeated. An enemy only stops attacking once he has won. If none of this sounds familiar, you may want to ask yourself or a close friend: am I even trying to walk faithfully with Jesus?

What is faith? The book of Hebrews tells us what it is and gives us an example of its results.

Now faith is the assurance of things hoped for, the conviction of things not seen (Hebrews 11:1).

By faith Moses, when he was grown up, refused to be called the son of Pharaoh's daughter, choosing rather to be mistreated with the people of God than to enjoy the fleeting pleasures of sin. He considered the reproach of Christ greater wealth than the treasures of Egypt, for he was looking to the reward. By faith he left Egypt, not being afraid of the anger of the king, for he endured as seeing him who is invisible (Hebrews 11:24-27).

Faith is a conviction and assurance about God. It is a wholehearted trust in God's character, in God's Word, and in Jesus as Lord and Savior. This faith will protect you from the evil one and this faith will be tested.

One of the great temptations in our lives is what the Bible calls "fear of man." We crave the approval of people around us and we fear what harm others can do to us. As the book of Hebrews tells us, Moses faced this fear in Egypt and overcame it by faith. How did he do so? Author Edward Welch provides an excellent answer.

"The most radical treatment for the fear of man is the fear of the Lord. God must be bigger to you than people are." [6]

How big is your shield? Well.... how big is your God? When you consider the various pressures upon you or the various desires you have, what looms bigger, other people or God? Do you spend time daily with the God of the universe through prayer and Scripture reading? If not, he may appear far smaller than the people you see every day at work, school, or home.

Salvation Isn't For Insurance; It's For Assurance
As a pastor, one of the more common questions I hear from Christians is this - How do I know I am saved?

Through many conversations with Christians about this question, I have come to realize something. The question being asked is not so much theological as it is practical. I know this because people are rarely satisfied with theological answers. Regardless of how much I explain and re-explain the Gospel of God's grace, they continue to ask the question. You see, it is extremely difficult for fallen human beings to get into their minds that God's grace cannot be earned. The question they are asking is a question of insurance. The problem is that salvation is not about insurance, but assurance.

After I have shared the Gospel with someone, one of the questions I will sometimes ask to check if they have understood it properly is this - "So, if you were to die today and stand before the pearly gates of heaven, and God were to ask, 'Why should I let you in?' What would you say?" Unfortunately, even after laying out the Gospel plainly, one of the answers I still frequently hear is this, "Well, I was a fairly good person."

For by grace you have been saved through faith. And this is not your own doing; it is the gift of God, not a result of works, so that no one may boast.
(Ephesians 2:8-9)

Even though the Bible is clear, we still want to believe we can earn our way into heaven.
The great preacher D. Martin Lloyd-Jones answered the question this way:

"Well then you ask, how may I know whether I am a Christian at all? The answer is that if you know you are a sinner; if you have ceased to rely upon your own good works; if you are looking only to the Lord Christ and His perfect work on your behalf - in His life, in his death upon the Cross, in His resurrection and ascension - if you are not looking at all to yourself; if you have no confidence in the flesh; if your only hope is in Him, and you are trusting in and relying utterly upon Him; then you are a Christian."[7]

A helmet is not a tool that you work with or on. A helmet is something you simply put on, close your eyes, and let it do its job. Scripture tells us to put on "for a helmet the hope of salvation. For God has not destined us for wrath, but to obtain salvation through our Lord Jesus Christ" (1 Thessalonians 5:8-9). Our assurance is not based upon our feelings or our works, but the fact of what Jesus Christ has done for us.

Another important word from D. Martin Lloyd-Jones:

"The supreme activity of the devil is upon the mind of man...One moment [the devil] comes to us, and tells us that we are not good enough to be Christians, another time he tells us we are so good that we do not need the death of Christ in order to save us."[8]

To put on the helmet of salvation is to have the Gospel clearly fixed in your mind. A helmet is an item you never forget you are wearing. You always feel it and notice it. The Christian should feel the same about their salvation through the Gospel.

For though we walk in the flesh, we are not waging war according to the flesh. For the weapons of our warfare are not of the flesh but have divine power to destroy strongholds. We destroy arguments and every lofty opinion raised against the knowledge of God, and take every thought captive to obey Christ (2 Corinthians 10:3-5).

So, what role do good works play then?

For by grace you have been saved through faith. And this is not your own doing; it is the gift of God, not a result of works, so that no one may boast. For we are his workmanship, created in Christ Jesus for good works, which God prepared beforehand, that we should walk in them (Ephesians 2:8-10).

The same passage that tells us forcefully that our salvation is not earned by works, goes on to tell us that good works must be the result of our salvation.

So, every healthy tree bears good fruit, but the diseased tree bears bad fruit. A healthy tree cannot bear bad fruit, nor can a diseased tree bear good fruit. Every tree that does not bear good fruit is cut down and thrown into the fire. Thus you will recognize them by their fruits (Matthew 7:17-20).

If you love me, you will keep my commandments (John 14:15).

Good works do not earn salvation, they are the result of salvation. They are not the root; they are the fruit. God first loved us and saved us. In response, we love him and our love overflows into obedience and good works.

God desires for us to have assurance, but this assurance is found by looking to Christ and not to ourselves.

I write these things to you who believe in the name of the Son of God, that you may know that you have eternal life (1 John 5:13).

Such knowledge is like a helmet that protects the Christian soldier.

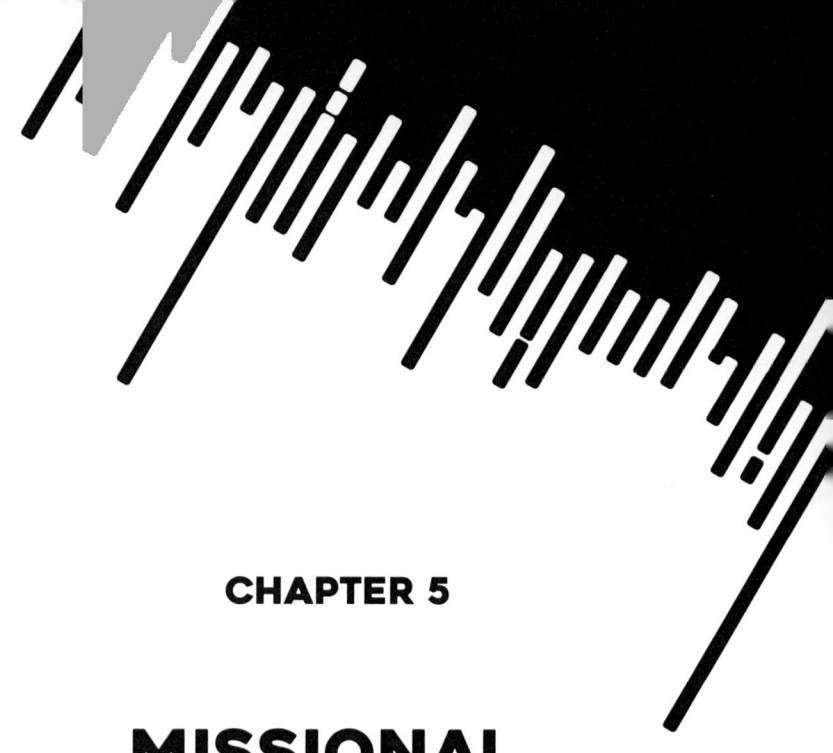

CHAPTER 5

MISSIONAL DECLINE VS THE WORD OF GOD

and the
sword of the Spirit,
which is the word of God,
praying at all times in the Spirit,
with all prayer and supplication. To that
end, keep alert with all perseverance, making
supplication for all the saints, and also for
me, that words may be given to me in opening
my mouth boldly to proclaim the mystery of
the Gospel, for which I am an ambassador
in chains, that I may declare it boldly, as
I ought to speak.
— *Ephesians 6:17-20*

Don't forget the assignment.

A recent study found that 75% of professing Christians couldn't explain the Great Commission.[9] At the same time, current demographic trends tell us that the number of Muslims in the United States will double by 2050, those who say they have no religion will be the majority in the United States by 2070, and Christianity will continue to decline.[10] [11] Perhaps the devil is advancing in his mission because Christians are confused or apathetic about theirs. The next generation of our country and local communities will be lost if Christians forget their assignment.

The Great Commission
All authority in heaven and on earth has been given to me. Go therefore and make disciples of all nations, baptizing them in the name of the Father and of the Son and of the Holy Spirit, teaching them to observe all that I have commanded you. And behold, I am with you always, to the end of the age.
(Matthew 28:18-20).

Advancing the mission doesn't mean you have to be a street evangelist or go to a third world country. God has called all of us to be on mission.

God's Truth Is How We Prevail

Up to this point, all the pieces of armor that we have discussed have been defensive. They are designed to help the Christian soldier withstand the attack of the enemy. There is only one item and the very last item mentioned that is designed for offense.

In high school, I had a football coach who pointed out the faulty logic of a common saying in sports - "defense wins games." He said, "Defense doesn't win games. Defense is important, but only a good offense will put enough points on the board to win the game."

The Christian soldier must stand against the attacks of the enemy. He or she must defend themselves from the lies of the world, the desires of the flesh, and the schemes of the devil. However, the Christian soldier is not only called to hold their ground, they are also called to go and take ground.

Let's breakdown the Great Commission passage (Matthew 28:18-20). In English, we see several verbs (action words) in the sentence, and it can look like the main command of the passage is to "go." However, in the original language, it is very clear that there is one main command and three supporting verbs. The main command of the Great Commission is to "make disciples." This main command is then further explained through three supporting verbs called participles (isn't grammar fun!?). So, the Great Commission really tells us to make disciples by going, baptizing, and teaching.

Withstand

So, let's eliminate any confusion about the mission of the Christian church. The mission is to make disciples of Jesus. What is a disciple? Most basically, a disciple is a learner or follower. The Bible has a lot to say about what it means to be a disciple (i.e. Matthew 16:24-26), but for now let's just look at what the Great Commission itself says. First, it says that a disciple is to be baptized into the name of our Triune God. This baptism depicts dying to our old life and beginning a new life that was given to us by God and is to be lived for God (Romans 6:4).

Second, the Great Commission says that a disciple is someone who is taught to obey God's commands. There are two key parts involved here, the teaching and the obeying, but both flow from one source. A disciple is someone who knows and obeys God's Word.

The preaching, teaching, and sharing of God's Word is how we gain ground. This is how disciples are made. This is how souls are snatched from the flames of hell. This is how our children are set on the right course. This is the sword of the Spirit.

For the word of God is living and active, sharper than any two-edged sword, piercing to the division of soul and of spirit, of joints and of marrow, and discerning the thoughts and intentions of the heart

(Hebrews 4:12).

Someone might ask: But I thought love was our weapon? I thought love was to be the defining factor of Christians and how we heap burning coals on the head of our enemies (Romans 12:20)? Love is certainly important. But love without truth is no love at all. The Bible tells us to speak the truth in love (Ephesians 4:15). We could say truth is the content, and love is the packaging. Or, to approach it from another angle, the most loving thing you can do is to tell someone the truth, especially eternal truth about life and death.

When Jesus faced down the devil, truth is how he prevailed (Matthew 4:1-11). He wielded the Sword of the Spirit. If we are not making the kind of disciples who can resist the devil by wielding the Word, then we are not doing the mission.

The Power Of The Spirit Through Prayer

The passage we have been studying throughout this book – a passage calling us to put on the armor of God – ends with a call to prayer.

...praying at all times in the Spirit, with all prayer and supplication (Ephesians 6:18).

How do we actually put on the armor of God? I think we have studied many practical answers to that question in this short book, but another simple answer would be to say: by prayer.

If the Word of God is the sword of the Spirit, it could be said that prayer is the radio of the Spirit. Prayer is how we communicate with our captain and king on the battlefield.

John Piper once put it this way:

"Prayer is primarily a wartime walkie-talkie for the mission of the church as it advances against the powers of darkness and unbelief. It is not surprising that prayer malfunctions when we try to make it a domestic intercom to call upstairs for more comforts in the den. God has given us prayer as a wartime walkie-talkie so that we can call headquarters for everything we need as the kingdom of Christ advances in the world."[12]

How do we pray in the Spirit as Scripture tells us (Ephesians 6:18)? Praying in the Spirit is not a magical experience or formula. This phrase refers to the power and the content of our prayers. The power of our prayer comes from the Spirit.

Likewise the Spirit helps us in our weakness. For we do not know what to pray for as we ought, but the Spirit himself intercedes for us with groanings too deep for words. And he who searches hearts knows what is the mind of the Spirit, because the Spirit intercedes for the saints according to the will of God (Romans 8:26-27).

Just as the power of our prayers comes from the Spirit, so should the content of our prayers be led by the Spirit. Our prayers should be in accord with the will of God and the mission of God. One great example is how Paul asks for prayer in Ephesians 6:19-20. He doesn't ask for comforts; he asks for words and boldness to proclaim the Gospel. This is a wartime prayer.

Brothers and sisters, pray for the advance of the Gospel in the world and for Christian growth in your own life, your family, and your church. Call in air support from high command. Ask the Lord to destroy enemy strongholds, to open people's eyes to the Gospel, and...pray that he would daily clothe you in his armor.

That in the day of evil you may be able to **withstand.**

Index

A
Apostasy 20
Assurance 42–44, 46, 48

B
Believe 13, 21, 26–27, 35, 45, 48

C
Christian soldier 9, 48, 52

D
D. Martin Lloyd-Jones 45–46
Devil 4–5, 8, 13–15, 19–22, 42, 46, 51–52
 Satan 4, 12–15, 21–23

E
Edward Welch 43
Eternity 20

F
Faith 4, 9, 27, 32, 40–43, 45, 47

G
Glory 4, 27
God's Word 43, 53
Good works 22, 27, 45, 47
Gossip 42

H
Heaven 31, 38, 51
Hell 12–13, 53

I
Image of God 2, 4, 22, 31

J
Jesus 2, 38, 42, 54
 as Lord and Savior 43
 Christ 16, 45–46
 created in 47
 disciples of 53
 lived the perfect life 27
 our faith in 9, 27
 peace with God through 32
 redemption that is in 27
 resurrection of 32
 returns 34
 righteousness 27
 salvation through 3, 10, 46
 Son 37
 the heart of 24
 through faith in 27, 32
John Piper 55

L

M
Law 23, 27

Muslims 51

P
Politics 31
Prayer 38, 42, 44, 50, 54–56
Preaching 37, 53

R
Righteous 18, 24, 26–27
Roman Empire 18
Roman soldier 21, 24, 32

S
Salvation 46–47
Scripture 19, 22, 32, 44, 46, 54–55
 1 Corinthians 15:1-8 32
 1 John 5:13 48
 1 Peter 5:8 14, 19

Index

1 Thessalonians 5:8-9 46
1 Timothy 4:1 4
1 Timothy 6:12 42
2 Corinthians 4:4 4
2 Corinthians 5:20 31
2 Corinthians 5:21 27
2 Corinthians 10:3-5 47
2 Timothy 2:3 9
2 Timothy 2:4 9
2 Timothy 4:3-4 3
2 Timothy 4:7 42
Bible 4, 11–12
Daniel 10 12
Daniel 10:12-14 12
Ephesians 2:8-9 45
Ephesians 2:8-10 27, 47
Ephesians 4:15 54
Ephesians 6:10-13 9
Ephesians 6:11 14
Ephesians 6:12 12, 14
Ephesians 6:14 18
Ephesians 6:15 30
Ephesians 6:16-17 40
Ephesians 6:17-20 50
Ephesians 6:18 54
Genesis 1:27 31
Hebrews 4:12 54
Hebrews 4:15 27
Hebrews 11:24-27 43
John 3:16 10
John 8:31-32 23
John 8:43-45 21
John 14:6 23
John 14:15 10, 47
Matthew 4:1-11 54
Matthew 7:17-20 47
Matthew 12:25 20
Matthew 16:24-26 53
Matthew 28:18-20 10, 51–52
Philippians 2:25 9
Psalm 1:1-2 23
Revelation 12:7-12 14
Romans 3:20-24 27
Romans 4:24-25 27
Romans 5:10 32
Romans 6:4 53
Romans 6:23 27
Romans 8:13 10
Romans 12:20 54
Sex 10–11, 35
Sin 3, 10, 23–27, 32, 42–43, 45
Spirit 4, 21, 37, 50–51, 53–56

End Notes

[1] Planned Parenthood. (2024, January 24). What is virginity? [Video]. YouTube. https://www.youtube.com/watch?v=ozhO62z2nag

[2] Brenan, M. (2023, July 20). Belief in five spiritual entities edges down to new lows. Gallup. https://news.gallup.com/poll/508886/belief-five-spiritual-entities-edges-down-new-lows.aspx

[3] Goodreads. (n.d.). Juvenal quotes [Quotes compilation]. Retrieved May 15, 2024, from https://www.goodreads.com/author/quotes/5838650.Juvenal#:~:text=The%20people%20that%20once%20bestowed,two%20things:%20bread%20and%20circuses!

[4] Newport, F. (2023, August 7). Update: Partisan gaps expand most on government power, climate. Gallup. https://news.gallup.com/poll/509129/update-partisan-gaps-expand-government-power-climate.aspx

[5] Jelly Roll. (2022). Whitsitt Chapel. Need a Favor. BBR.

[6] Welch, E. (1997). When people are big and God is small. P&R Publishing.

[7] Martyn Lloyd-Jones, D. (1976a). The Christian Warfare. Baker Books.

[8] Martyn Lloyd-Jones, D. (1976b). The Christian warfare. Baker Books.

[9] Barna. (2018, March 27). 51% of churchgoers don't know of the Great Commission. Barna. https://www.barna.com/research/half-churchgoers-not-heard-great-commission

[10] Mohamed, B. (2016, January 6). A new estimate of the U.S. Muslim population. Pew Research Center. https://www.pewresearch.org/short-reads/2016/01/06/a-new-estimate-of-the-u-s-muslim-population

[11] Pew Research Center. (2022, September 13). Projecting U.S. religious groups' population shares by 2070. Pew Research Center. https://www.pewresearch.org/religion/2022/09/13/projecting-us-religious-groups-population-shares-by-2070

[12] Piper, J. (1993). Let the nations be glad. Baker Academic.

RESOUND

BLOGS | PODCASTS | VIDEOS

RESOUNDMEDIA.CC